TRIBES of NATIVE AMERICA

Pima

edited by Marla Felkins Ryan
and Linda Schmittroth

BLACKBIRCH®
PRESS

THOMSON
GALE

San Diego • Detroit • New York • San Francisco • Cleveland
New Haven, Conn. • Waterville, Maine • London • Munich

THOMSON

GALE

For more information, contact
The Gale Group, Inc.
27500 Drake Rd.
Farmington Hills, MI 48331-3535
Or you can visit our Internet site at http://www.gale.com

Photo credits: Cover Courtesy of Northwestern University Library; cover © National Archives; cover © Photospin; cover © Perry Jasper Photography; cover © Picturequest; cover © Seattle Post-Intelligencer Collection, Museum of History & Industry; cover © PhotoDisc; cover © Library of Congress; pages 5 (both), 10, 12, 13, 17, 19, 20, 22, 23 (top), 24 (both), 25, 27 (bottom), 28, 29 © Marilyn "Angel" Wynn, nativestock.com; page 7 © N. Carter/North Wind Picture Archives; pages 9, 11 © North Wind Picture Archives; page 3, 23 (bottom) © Library of Congress; pages 6, 31 (bottom) © Corel Corporation; page 16 © Ken Levine/AP Wide World; page 30 © J. Pat Carter/ AP Wide World; page 14 © Bettmann/CORBIS; page 15 © Lowell Georgia/CORBIS; page 26 © Arne Hodalic/CORBIS; page 21 © Denver Public Library, Western History Collection, X-32552; page 31 (top) © National Archives; page 27 (top) © Hulton|Archive/Getty Images

LIBRARY OF CONGRESS CATALOGING-IN-PUBLICATION DATA

Pima / Marla Felkins Ryan, book editor ; Linda Schmittroth, book editor.

v. cm. — (Tribes of Native America)
Includes bibliographical references and index.
Contents: Name — History — Government — Daily life — Current tribal issues.
ISBN 1-56711-699-X (alk. paper)
1. Pima Indians—History—Juvenile literature. 2. Pima Indians—Social life and customs—Juvenile literature. [1. Pima Indians. 2. Indians of North America—Southwest, New.] I. Ryan, Marla Felkins. II. Schmittroth, Linda. III. Series.

E99.P6P56 2004
979.1004'9745—dc21

2003002631

Table of Contents

PIMA

Name

Pima (pronounced *PEE-mah*). The Pima called
themselves *Akimel Oodham* or *Akimel Au-Authm,*
which means the "river people." When Spanish
explorers first met the tribe, they asked the Indians
many questions. The Indians answered *Pi-nyi-match,* or
"I do not know," to each question. The Spanish
misunderstood and thought the Indians said *Pima.*
After that, the Spanish explorers called them the Pima.

Contemporary
Communities
Arizona
1. Gila River Pima-Maricopa
   Indian Community
2. Salt River Pima-Maricopa
   Indian Community
3. Ak-Chin Indian
   Community
Shaded area: Traditional
lands of the Pima in the
Sonoran Desert in present-
day southern Arizona,
southeastern California, and
northern Mexico

NEVADA

UTAH

ARIZONA

NEW
MEXICO

MEXICO

NORTH AMERICA

Pima

Pacific
Ocean

Gulf of
Mexico

Atlantic Ocean

The Pima and their descendants, like the basket dancers pictured here, made their homes in the Sonoran Desert.

Where are the traditional Pima lands?

The Pima were desert dwellers. They lived in many parts of the vast Sonoran Desert. The Upper Pimans lived in southern Arizona and southeastern California. The Lower Pimans lived in western Sonora. Today, the descendants of the Upper Pimans live with members of the Maricopa tribe. The tribes live on the Gila River Reservation and the Salt River Reservation in southern Arizona. Some Pima also live on the Ak-Chin Reservation in Maricopa, Arizona. (Today, Lower Pimans are called Tohono Oodham.)

The Gila River Reservation's cultural center and museum (below) offers visitors a glimpse of the Pima's rich history and way of life.

The Pima inhabited the Sonoran Desert before the first Spanish explorers arrived.

What has happened to the population?

In 1694 there were about 2,000 to 3,000 Pima. In a 1990 population count by the U.S. Bureau of the Census, 15,074 people said they were Pima.

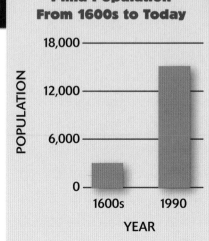

Pima Population From 1600s to Today

POPULATION

18,000

12,000

6,000

0

1600s   1990

YEAR

Origins and group ties

The Pima claim to have first lived in the Salt River valley. Later, they moved to the Gila River area. They are probably descended from the prehistoric Hohokam people, whose culture had faded by about 1450. The Pima Nation shares a similar language and certain traits with tribes in Sonora, Mexico. The Pima were friends and allies of the Maricopa. They were enemies of the Apache, who often raided and stole from them.

The Pima were farmers. They learned modern ways to farm from the Spanish. Soon afterward, they became wealthy farmers. Their new wealth changed them from a gentle people into warriors. They were forced to protect their surplus crops from enemy raiders. The Pima often traded their crops to American settlers who passed through their desert lands. Present-day Pima continue to farm the dry lands of Arizona. Modern technology has made it easier to water their farms.

Remnants of the Hohokam, possible ancestors of the Pima, still exist in the Sonoran Desert.

HISTORY

Early encounters with the Spanish

It is unknown how long the Pima Indians have lived in Arizona and Mexico. When the Spanish first met them in 1694, the Pima had already learned to survive in the many different environments of their homeland. Some of their lands were very dry, so there was little food or water. In other areas, crops grew strong. The Pima lived in several farming communities. The people worked together to plant and harvest crops.

When the Spanish first made contact with them, the Pima were weak. For 170 years the Pima had suffered from outbreaks of diseases. After their arrival in the New World, the Spanish tried to convert many tribes to the Catholic faith. They wanted to make the Indians a useful part of the Spanish empire. Tribes such as the Pueblo rebelled against the Spanish. Because their land was far off from other tribes, the Pima had little contact with outsiders. They were too busy with their farms to join revolts.

The Spanish government liked the way the Pima worked hard on their farms. The Spanish were also happy that the Pima did not join in the

Spanish missionaries attempted to convert the Indians to Catholicism.

many native revolts that occurred in the eighteenth century. The Spanish wanted to win the tribe's help, so they taught the Indians some modern ways to farm.

Spanish advances make wealthy farmers

Pima farms soon benefited from Spanish farming advances. The tribe gained a new food crop called winter wheat, which allowed them to farm

1871
New non-Indian settlements reduce the water supply to Pima lands, which destroys the tribe's farms

1879
Salt River Indian Reservation is created

1895
Congress formally establishes the Gila River Indian Community, and 375,000 acres of land are set aside for Native Americans

1917–1918
World War I fought in Europe

1941
Bombing at Pearl Harbor forces United States into World War II

1945
World War II ends

1950s
Reservations no longer controlled by federal government

1989–1990
The National Museum of the American Indian Act and the Native American Grave Protection and Reparations Act bring about the return of burial remains to native tribes

The Pima benefited from tools, like the grinding stone pictured here, which were introduced by the Spanish.

year-round. They learned how to grow more food when they used the Spanish methods to water crops. Years of success followed.

Because the tribe had extra grain and cotton, it could trade for other goods. When the Apache saw how much the Pima had gained, they began to raid Pima communities. Small groups of Pima moved into larger settlements for protection. The Pima began to sharpen their skills as fighters.

In 1848, after the American victory in the Mexican-American War, the United States gained Pima lands. The Pima hoped to learn how the Americans farmed their lands. They were disappointed when no such help was given. For their part, the Pima proved to be good friends to the United States. They traded food and farm animals to pioneers who traveled through Pima lands during the California gold rush. They also helped the U.S. Army protect settlers against

Apache raiders. They traded farm goods to U.S. troops. The Pima hoped to receive guns and shovels in return for their help. They were deeply offended when the U.S. government failed to deliver on its promises. The tribe's anger and confusion grew when the federal government gave farming tools to the Pima's traditional enemy, the Apache. (The Apache did not farm, so the tools were probably not even used.)

To protect themselves from Apache raids, the Pima moved from their small villages to larger settlements.

The land of the Salt River Pima-Maricopa Indian Community Reservation was too dry to farm.

Around the same time, the Apache led raids on Maricopa villages to the west. The attacks forced the Maricopa to move onto Pima territory. In 1859 American surveyors plotted out a reservation for both the Pima and Maricopa. It was called the Salt River Pima-Maricopa Indian Community Reservation. The reservation included only fields but no water. The era of Pima farming wealth quickly began to fade.

A way of life disappears

In 1871 a dam was built that diverted water from the Gila River to land settled by whites. Without water, the Pima could no longer farm. Some Pima moved south to settle near the Salt River. In 1879 their new settlement became the Salt River Indian Reservation.

The traditional Pima way of life disappeared completely between 1871 and 1914. Some Pima did physical labor for whites to earn money. Presbyterian missionaries did not allow the Pima to practice their traditional religion. The missionaries took over the education of Pima children. Tensions within the tribe grew. Isolated from the world, the Pima did not want to learn English or adopt white ways. The people fell into poverty and despair.

Missionaries taught Pima children and made them follow the Presbyterian religion.

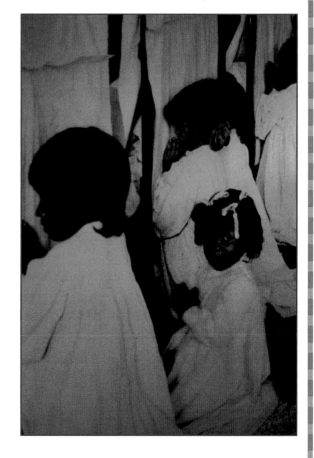

Becoming a part of the outside world

At the start of the twentieth century, the Pima had almost no contact with the outside world. They became less isolated after they acquired battery-powered radios and began to learn English. Some Pima men served in the U.S. military during World War II (1939–1945). They returned to the reservations determined to lead their fellow Pima into modern life.

In the first half of the twentieth century, major waterway projects diverted some water back to Pima land. Since then, the Pima have benefited from the economic growth of nearby urban areas. Today, Pima leaders work hard to meet the challenges of the twenty-first century. They want the tribe to adopt worthwhile aspects of American culture. They want to help Pima farms keep up with the competition. In addition, they want the tribe to find more ways to earn money besides the farms.

In the twentieth century, dams (pictured) and other waterway projects guided water back to Pima land.

Religion

Not much is known about the early Pima religion. In the Pima origin story, the Earthmaker created a world that was lived in by supernatural beings such as Coyote the trickster and a man-eating beast. A great flood caused the supernatural beings to flee. Elder Brother returned to create the Pima and their neighbors. Like other Southwestern Indians, the Pima celebrated the corn harvest and rainmaking.

Early Spanish Catholic missionaries had little influence on the Pima. The people accepted a few Catholic rituals, such as baptism. These rituals were blended with traditional Pima ceremonies. Presbyterian missionaries arrived during the 1870s. They had a strong impact on the Pima. By the 1890s, they claimed about eighteen hundred Pima as members. Officials of the Catholic Church returned and started the first missions

The Pima believed that these giant rock columns represent supernatural beings that fled the earth before humans came into being.

among the Pima around 1900. The tribe was not happy with this new attempt to convert them to another kind of Christianity.

Government

Long ago, the Pima lived in independent farming communities. Each one had its own leader and one or two shamans (pronounced *SHAH-munz* or *SHAY-munz*). The shaman's job was to heal the sick, control the weather, and promise success in battle. As the Pima began to interact more with outsiders through trade and warfare, the job of leader became more important. The job was soon passed down from father to son.

In the late twentieth century the Pima lived on reservations held jointly with the Maricopa, an old neighbor and ally. The Gila River Indian Community is governed by a seventeen-member elected tribal council. It has a governor and a lieutenant governor. The Salt River tribe is governed by the Salt River Pima-Maricopa Indian Community Council. Its seven elected members include a president and a vice president.

The Salt River Pima-Maricopa Indian Community Council represents the Salt River Pima in tribe-related signing ceremonies (pictured).

Economy

The Pima have always been farmers. They became traders only after the Spanish arrived in the New World. The Pima did not always buy and sell goods the way that white settlers did. At one time, they gave most items as gifts. In this system of give-and-take, a person offered something to another person who had to accept it. The giver gained power or importance. The person who received the gift was expected to return the gift in some way. Sometimes, the gift-giver used lines to mark the value of a gift. For example, when grains or beans were put in a basket, lines were drawn on the basket to mark how

Prior to the arrival of the Spanish, the Pima used gift baskets (pictured) to exchange goods.

high up the side the grain or beans came. This was done so that when an item was returned in the basket, it matched or exceeded the original in worth.

After contact with the Spanish, the Pima began to grow winter wheat and use better methods to water crops. They were able to grow even more crops. The new farming methods allowed the Pima to trade their extra grain with other tribes and with nonnatives. Eventually, the Pima sold their crops for gold and silver.

Because the Pima had become very well off, the tribe was often attacked by Apache raiders. To get back at the Apache thieves, the Pima sometimes kidnapped Apache children. The children were sold to the Spanish for use as slaves. The Pima later traded wheat, baskets, and blankets to the Mexicans and other tribes for items such as animal skins and wild peppers.

At one time, the Pima grew only as much food as the tribe needed. Later, they needed to grow more crops because so many groups wanted to buy their grains. With their new wealth, tribe members could gain personal possessions. By the time the Pima lost the water they needed to grow extra crops, they had also lost the old ways to farm their land. They had forgotten how to work together and share their harvests. Nearly one hundred years passed before the tribe could farm productively again.

A water crisis hit tribal lands in the late 1800s. Afterward, some Pima were forced to turn to jobs that paid little money. Some went on government welfare. The reservations tried to find new ways to use their land. Some land was leased to outside industries, such as a brass foundry and a telecommunications business. These companies brought jobs to the reservations.

With modern watering techniques in practice, agriculture is once again an important source of income for the Pima. In addition to their fine Pima cotton, the tribe harvests crops such as wheat, alfalfa, melons, olives, and citrus fruits. The tribe also benefits from tourism to the area. There are golf courses, an international race park, and many tribal events that are open to the public.

Golf courses and other developments attract tourists to tribal lands, and provide the Pima with an important source of income.

PIMA COTTON: AMONG THE WORLD'S FINEST

Extra-long staple (ELS) cotton has been grown in the Southwest since the early 1900s. It was once called American-Egyptian cotton. In 1951 a seed was developed that produced a superior ELS cotton. This cotton is known for its outstanding silkiness. It was called Pima cotton in honor of the Pima. The Pima had grown the cotton on a U.S. Department of Agriculture experimental farm in Sacaton, Arizona. Pima cotton is used by the world's finest mills to make cloth.

Manufacturers around the world use Pima cotton to make high-quality goods.

DAILY LIFE

Families

Most Pima families had a husband and wife, their young children, the families of their married sons, and their unmarried adult daughters.

The wife and children of a Pima man joined his parents' family.

Buildings

The early Pima built small, round houses with flat roofs. The house was called a *ki* (pronounced kee). The typical *ki* was 10 to 25 feet across. The wooden frame was covered with reeds, straw, or cornstalks. Dirt was then put over the plants or straw. Four wooden posts and two main support beams propped up the roof. The support beams, in turn, braced several lighter cross poles. Light willow poles were bent in a circle around this square frame and tied to it. Although they often leaked, these homes could survive strong winds.

A traditional Pima village also had a rectangular council house and storehouses. Arbors were made from cottonwood to protect people from the heat of the sun.

The Pima lived in *ki*-style single-family homes until the late 1800s. The tribe began to build pueblo-style adobe (pronounced uh-DOE-bee) houses around the turn of the twentieth century. Later, cement-block construction became popular.

Pima families lived in a *ki* (pictured) until the late nineteenth century.

The Pima wore simple clothing like the cotton garments pictured here.

Clothing

Before the Spanish arrived in Pima territory, the tribe wore little clothing. Men dressed in breechcloths. These garments had front and back flaps that hung from the waist. Women usually wore cotton skirts. The skirts were padded to make them stand away from the body. Sandals and cotton blankets added protection and warmth when needed. Later on, Pima men wore Spanish clothing as a sign of their importance.

Pima men added hair and cloth to make unique hairstyles.

The Pima spent a lot of time on their hairstyles. Men and women wore their hair long. Women wore their hair loose with bangs. Men braided or twisted their hair into locks. They added human or horse hair and headbands to create a bulky mass they considered attractive. Frequent brushings and a dressing made of river mud and mesquite gum kept their hair dark and shiny. The Pima sometimes painted their hair, faces, and bodies. Both men and women had their lower

eyelids lined with tattoos, usually at the time of puberty or marriage. Men also tattooed lines across their foreheads. Women added lines along each side of the chin.

Food

For many centuries, Pima farmers used only two tools: a digging stick and a sharpened piece of wood that served as both hoe and harvester. They farmed the islands in the Gila River and the land on the nearby floodplain. The tribe's most important crops were corn and tepary (pronounced *TEH-puh-ree*) beans. They also ate wild foods such as mesquite beans and saguaro (*suh-WAHR-uh*) cactus fruit.

Although their methods were primitive, the Pima usually harvested enough food so they did not need to hunt or gather. When drought or other catastrophes damaged their crops, they hunted and searched for food to make up for the lost crops.

Fruit plucked from saguaros (left) and beans from mesquite trees (right) were part of the Pima diet.

In the early reservation period, Pima children received their education from missionaries and government agents.

Education

In early times, Pima chiefs and parents were a child's most important source of knowledge. Their role was taken over by missionaries and government agents during the early reservation period.

Present-day Pima want their children to have an education so that they will have good jobs. Education starts early with a Head Start program for preschoolers. There are elementary schools on the reservations. Young people go to public high schools in nearby cities. Pima children are encouraged to attend college and to return home with their new skills to improve life in the tribe.

Pima shamans communicated with spirits to help heal sick members of the tribe.

Healing practices

The early Pima believed that people could become ill if they behaved badly toward animals. They could also become sick if they offended clouds or lightning. Sick people called on shaman-healers for help. Shamans gained their powers through dream visions. In these dreams, they met powerful supernatural beings. Later, they could call upon these beings to help heal the sick.

To find out what made a person sick, the shaman breathed tobacco smoke over the patient's body. Sometimes, he used an eagle feather or crystal to connect with the spirit world. This ritual allowed the shaman to see what spirits had visited the body and harmed its health. If these steps did not work, the shaman sang to the spirits. In his song, he asked the spirits to tell him more about the illness. Then, he could do a ritual to cure the person.

The Pima thought of shamans as heroes. When white missionaries arrived, they told the Indians not to trust the shamans. Because of this, three shamans were blamed for the outbreak of a terrible illness. The Pima killed the shamans. In the late twentieth century, shamans regained the respect once given to them. By this time, there were far fewer shamans.

Arts

The Pima made beautiful baskets. They also wove attractive cotton blankets. Their pottery was ordinary in style. It was more useful than decorative.

The Pima wove baskets with striking designs.

Pima pottery was useful in everyday life.

CUSTOMS

Festivals and ceremonies

In the old times, the Pima had only a few ceremonies. Modern Pima celebrate many occasions. One annual festival is the New Year's Chicken Scratch Dance. The Mul-Chu-Tha is a tribal fair that raises money for youth activities. It features a parade, Indian rodeo, arts and crafts, and dances. Each year, the tribe has a traditional song-and-dance celebration called the Red Mountain Eagle Powwow. Modern-day powwows include singers and dancers from many different tribes.

Modern-day Pima celebrate many more occasions than their ancestors did.

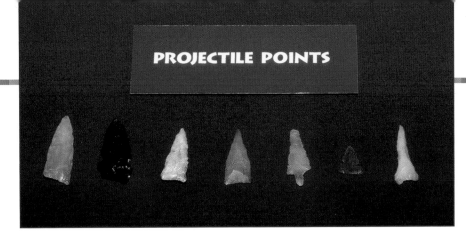

PROJECTILE POINTS

To make their weapons even more deadly, Pima warriors put rattlesnake poison on the points (pictured).

War rituals

The early Pima were a gentle people who wanted peace. The wealth they gained from the trade of their extra crops changed their lives. They were forced to defend themselves from raids by tribes who wanted what they had. Wars became more frequent once the tribe began to fight back against the thieves. The Pima trained their men to be fierce warriors. They fought with heavy clubs and shot arrows treated with rattlesnake poison. Although they fought, the Pima still believed that war was evil. When a Pima warrior killed someone, he tried to make up for the person's death. He went away for a sixteen-day purification, or cleansing ceremony. The ritual involved a fast. A shaman performed special rites to cleanse the warrior's weapons.

Marriage and divorce

Parents usually arranged marriages for their children. The children could freely express their wishes about their future mates. Marriages in Pima society were very informal. The couple lived together and declared themselves married. There was no ceremony to mark the occasion. Divorce and remarriage were also simple matters.

Current tribal issues

Like other Southwestern tribes today, the Pima work hard to improve education and health care on their reservations. Many Southwest tribes have partially closed their communities to outsiders. They want to protect some of their culture through secrecy. The Pima do not close off their communities. The tribe allows outsiders to observe their culture. Modern Pima have held onto their history and traditions, despite outside attempts to change them.

Reservation hospitals like this one are part of the Pima's ongoing effort to improve health care.

Notable people

Ira Hamilton Hayes (1923–1955) was the most famous Native American soldier of World War II. In February 1945 his military group landed on Iwo Jima. The United States used this island in the Pacific Ocean to launch air strikes against Japan. Hayes was one of six marines who raised the U.S. flag there in the middle of heavy enemy fire. The photograph of that heroic act became famous. After he finished his military service, Hayes returned to the Pima reservation. The fame he gained as a war hero had a destructive effect on him. He became a drifter, an alcoholic, and a lawbreaker. Hayes died of exposure in the Arizona desert on January 24, 1955.

Ira Hamilton Hayes, a Pima and U.S. marine, gained fame in World War II.

For more information

Ezell, Paul H., "History of the Pima." *Handbook of North American Indians,* vol. 10: *Southwest.* Alfonso Ortiz, ed. Washington, DC: Smithsonian Institution Press, 1983.

Innis, Gilbert C., "Pima." *Native America in the Twentieth Century.* Mary B. Davis, ed. New York: Garland, 1994.

Russell, Frank, *The Pima Indians.* Tucson: University of Arizona Press, 1975.

This statue immortalizes Hayes and the other marines who raised the flag at Iwo Jima.

Glossary

Adobe a heavy clay used to make bricks for buildings

Ki **(kee)** a small, round Pima house with a flat roof

Missionary a person on a religious mission to convert other people to his faith

Mul-Chu-Tha a Pima tribal fair that raises money for youth activities

Pima cotton a superior type of cotton named after the Pima tribe

Powwow a Native American gathering or ceremony

Reservation land set aside for Native Americans by the government

Saguaro (suh-wahr-uh) a type of cactus plant

Shaman a Native American priest who used magic to heal people and see the future

Tepary a type of bean

Index